Date _____ Caster _____

Name of Ritual or Spell _____

Purpose _____

Participants   Deities Invoked

Waxing   Full Moon   Waning

Description

Ingredients and Equipment

Immediate feelings and effects

Follow Up

Manifestation Date _____

Results _____

Date _____ Caster _____

Name of Ritual or Spell _____

Purpose _____

Participants   **Deities Invoked**

| Waxing | Full Moon | Waning |

Description

Ingredients and Equipment

Immediate feelings and effects

Follow Up

Manifestation Date _____

Results _____

Date _____ Caster _____

Name of Ritual or Spell _____

Purpose _____

Participants   Deities Invoked

| Waxing | Full Moon | Waning |

Description

Ingredients and Equipment

Immediate feelings and effects

Follow Up

Manifestation Date _____

Results _____

Date _____   Caster _____

Name of Ritual or Spell _____

Purpose _____

Participants   **Deities Invoked**

| Waxing | | | Full Moon | | | Waning |

Description

Ingredients and Equipment

Immediate feelings and effects

Follow Up

Manifestation Date _____

Results _____

Date _____ Caster _____

Name of Ritual or Spell _____

Purpose _____

Participants   **Deities Invoked**

| Waxing | Full Moon | Waning |

Description

Ingredients and Equipment

Immediate feelings and effects

Follow Up

Manifestation Date _____

Results _____

Date _____ Caster _____

Name of Ritual or Spell _____

Purpose _____

Participants   **Deities Invoked**

Waxing   Full Moon   Waning

Description

Ingredients and Equipment

Immediate feelings and effects

Follow Up

Manifestation Date _____

Results _____

Date _____   Caster _____

Name of Ritual or Spell _____

Purpose _____

Participants   Deities Invoked

| Waxing | Full Moon | Waning |

Description

Ingredients and Equipment

Immediate feelings and effects

Follow Up

Manifestation Date _____

Results _____

Date _____ Caster _____

Name of Ritual or Spell _____

Purpose _____

Participants   Deities Invoked

Waxing	Full Moon	Waning

Description

Ingredients and Equipment

Immediate feelings and effects

Follow Up

Manifestation Date _____

Results _____

Date _____ Caster _____

Name of Ritual or Spell _____

Purpose _____

Participants   Deities Invoked

Waxing   Full Moon   Waning

Description

Ingredients and Equipment

Immediate feelings and effects

Follow Up

Manifestation Date _____

Results _____

Date _____ Caster _____

Name of Ritual or Spell _____

Purpose _____

Participants   Deities Invoked

Waxing   Full Moon   Waning

Description

Ingredients and Equipment

Immediate feelings and effects

Follow Up

Manifestation Date _____

Results _____

Date _____ Caster _____

Name of Ritual or Spell _____

Purpose _____

Participants   Deities Invoked

Waxing   Full Moon   Waning

Description

Ingredients and Equipment

Immediate feelings and effects

Follow Up

Manifestation Date _____

Results _____

Date _____ Caster _____

Name of Ritual or Spell _____

Purpose _____

Participants   **Deities Invoked**

Waxing   Full Moon   Waning

Description

Ingredients and Equipment

Immediate feelings and effects

Follow Up

Manifestation Date _____

Results _____

Date _____ Caster _____

Name of Ritual or Spell _____

Purpose _____

Participants   Deities Invoked

| Waxing | Full Moon | Waning |

Description

Ingredients and Equipment

Immediate feelings and effects

Follow Up

Manifestation Date _____

Results _____

Date _____   Caster _____

Name of Ritual or Spell _____

Purpose _____

Participants   **Deities Invoked**

Waxing   Full Moon   Waning

Description

Ingredients and Equipment

Immediate feelings and effects

Follow Up

Manifestation Date _____

Results _____

Date _____ Caster _____

Name of Ritual or Spell _____

Purpose _____

Participants   Deities Invoked

| Waxing | Full Moon | Waning |

Description

Ingredients and Equipment

Immediate feelings and effects

Follow Up

Manifestation Date _____

Results _____

Date _____ Caster _____

Name of Ritual or Spell _____

Purpose _____

Participants   Deities Invoked

Waxing			Full Moon		Waning	

Description

Ingredients and Equipment

Immediate feelings and effects

Follow Up

Manifestation Date _____

Results _____

Date _____ Caster _____

Name of Ritual or Spell _____

Purpose _____

Participants   Deities Invoked

| Waxing | Full Moon | Waning |

Description

Ingredients and Equipment

Immediate feelings and effects

Follow Up

Manifestation Date _____

Results _____

Date _____   Caster _____

Name of Ritual or Spell _____

Purpose _____

Participants   **Deities Invoked**

Waxing	Full Moon	Waning

Description

Ingredients and Equipment

Immediate feelings and effects

Follow Up

Manifestation Date _____

Results _____

Date _____ Caster _____

Name of Ritual or Spell _____

Purpose _____

Participants   Deities Invoked

| Waxing | Full Moon | Waning |

Description

Ingredients and Equipment

Immediate feelings and effects

Follow Up

Manifestation Date _____

Results _____

Date _____   Caster _____

Name of Ritual or Spell _____

Purpose _____

Participants   **Deities Invoked**

Waxing	Full Moon	Waning

Description

Ingredients and Equipment

Immediate feelings and effects

Follow Up

Manifestation Date _____

Results _____

Date _____ Caster _____

Name of Ritual or Spell _____

Purpose _____

Participants   Deities Invoked

| Waxing | Full Moon | Waning |

Description

Ingredients and Equipment

Immediate feelings and effects

Follow Up

Manifestation Date _____

Results _____

Date _____ Caster _____

Name of Ritual or Spell _____

Purpose _____

Participants   Deities Invoked

Waxing	Full Moon	Waning

Description

_____
_____
_____
_____

Ingredients and Equipment

_____
_____
_____
_____
_____
_____
_____
_____
_____
_____

Immediate feelings and effects

_____
_____
_____
_____
_____

Follow Up

Manifestation Date _____

Results _____

Date _____   Caster _____

Name of Ritual or Spell _____

Purpose _____

Participants   Deities Invoked

| Waxing | | | Full Moon | | Waning | |

| Description | | Ingredients and Equipment |

| Immediate feelings and effects | | |

Follow Up

Manifestation Date _____

Results _____

Date _____   Caster _____

Name of Ritual or Spell _____

Purpose _____

Participants   **Deities Invoked**

Waxing	Full Moon	Waning

Description

Ingredients and Equipment

Immediate feelings and effects

Follow Up

Manifestation Date _____

Results _____

Date _____ Caster _____

Name of Ritual or Spell _____

Purpose _____

Participants **Deities Invoked**

| Waxing | Full Moon | Waning |

Description

Ingredients and Equipment

Immediate feelings and effects

Follow Up

Manifestation Date _____

Results _____

Date _____ Caster _____

Name of Ritual or Spell _____

Purpose _____

Participants **Deities Invoked**

Waxing   Full Moon   Waning

Description

_____
_____
_____
_____

Ingredients and Equipment

_____
_____
_____
_____
_____
_____
_____
_____

Immediate feelings and effects

_____
_____
_____
_____

Follow Up

Manifestation Date _____

Results _____

Date _____ Caster _____

Name of Ritual or Spell _____

Purpose _____

Participants   Deities Invoked

Waxing	Full Moon	Waning

Description

Ingredients and Equipment

Immediate feelings and effects

Follow Up

Manifestation Date _____

Results _____

Date _____   Caster _____

Name of Ritual or Spell _____

Purpose _____

Participants   **Deities Invoked**

Waxing   Full Moon   Waning

Description

Ingredients and Equipment

Immediate feelings and effects

Follow Up

Manifestation Date _____

Results _____

Date _____ Caster _____

Name of Ritual or Spell _____

Purpose _____

Participants   Deities Invoked

| Waxing | Full Moon | Waning |

Description

Ingredients and Equipment

Immediate feelings and effects

Follow Up

Manifestation Date _____

Results _____

Date _____ Caster _____

Name of Ritual or Spell _____

Purpose _____

Participants **Deities Invoked**

| Waxing | Full Moon | Waning |

Description

Ingredients and Equipment

Immediate feelings and effects

Follow Up

Manifestation Date _____

Results _____

Date _____ Caster _____

Name of Ritual or Spell _____

Purpose _____

Participants   Deities Invoked

| Waxing | Full Moon | Waning |

Description

Ingredients and Equipment

Immediate feelings and effects

Follow Up

Manifestation Date _____

Results _____

Date _____ Caster _____

Name of Ritual or Spell _____

Purpose _____

Participants   **Deities Invoked**

| Waxing | Full Moon | Waning |

Description

Ingredients and Equipment

Immediate feelings and effects

Follow Up

Manifestation Date _____

Results _____

Date _____ Caster _____

Name of Ritual or Spell _____

Purpose _____

Participants   Deities Invoked

| Waxing | Full Moon | Waning |

Description

Ingredients and Equipment

Immediate feelings and effects

Follow Up

Manifestation Date _____

Results _____

Date _____ Caster _____

Name of Ritual or Spell _____

Purpose _____

Participants   **Deities Invoked**

Waxing   Full Moon   Waning

Description

Ingredients and Equipment

Immediate feelings and effects

Follow Up

Manifestation Date _____

Results _____

Date _____ Caster _____

Name of Ritual or Spell _____

Purpose _____

Participants   Deities Invoked

| Waxing | Full Moon | Waning |

Description

Ingredients and Equipment

Immediate feelings and effects

Follow Up

Manifestation Date _____

Results _____

Date _____ Caster _____

Name of Ritual or Spell _____

Purpose _____

Participants   **Deities Invoked**

Waxing	Full Moon	Waning

Description

Ingredients and Equipment

Immediate feelings and effects

Follow Up

Manifestation Date _____

Results _____

Date _____ Caster _____

Name of Ritual or Spell _____

Purpose _____

Participants   Deities Invoked

| Waxing | Full Moon | Waning |

Description

Ingredients and Equipment

Immediate feelings and effects

Follow Up

Manifestation Date _____

Results _____

Date _____ Caster _____

Name of Ritual or Spell _____

Purpose _____

Participants　　　　　**Deities Invoked**

| Waxing | Full Moon | Waning |

Description

Ingredients and Equipment

Immediate feelings and effects

Follow Up

Manifestation Date _____

Results _____

Date _____ Caster _____

Name of Ritual or Spell _____

Purpose _____

Participants   Deities Invoked

Waxing   Full Moon   Waning

Description

Ingredients and Equipment

Immediate feelings and effects

Follow Up

Manifestation Date _____

Results _____

Date _____ Caster _____

Name of Ritual or Spell _____

Purpose _____

Participants   Deities Invoked

Waxing	Full Moon	Waning

Description

Ingredients and Equipment

Immediate feelings and effects

Follow Up

Manifestation Date _____

Results _____

Date _____ **Caster** _____

Name of Ritual or Spell _____

Purpose _____

Participants   Deities Invoked

| Waxing | Full Moon | Waning |

Description

Ingredients and Equipment

Immediate feelings and effects

Follow Up

Manifestation Date _____

Results _____

Date _____   Caster _____

Name of Ritual or Spell _____

Purpose _____

Participants   **Deities Invoked**

Waxing	Full Moon	Waning

Description

Ingredients and Equipment

Immediate feelings and effects

Follow Up

Manifestation Date _____

Results _____

Date _____   Caster _____

Name of Ritual or Spell _____

Purpose _____

Participants   Deities Invoked

| Waxing | Full Moon | Waning |

Description

Ingredients and Equipment

Immediate feelings and effects

Follow Up

Manifestation Date _____

Results _____

Date _____   Caster _____

Name of Ritual or Spell _____

Purpose _____

Participants   **Deities Invoked**

Waxing   Full Moon   Waning

Description

Ingredients and Equipment

Immediate feelings and effects

Follow Up

Manifestation Date _____

Results _____

Date _____ Caster _____

Name of Ritual or Spell _____

Purpose _____

Participants   Deities Invoked

Waxing			Full Moon			Waning

Description

Ingredients and Equipment

Immediate feelings and effects

Follow Up

Manifestation Date _____

Results _____

Date _____   Caster _____

Name of Ritual or Spell _____

Purpose _____

Participants   Deities Invoked

| Waxing | Full Moon | Waning |

Description

Ingredients and Equipment

Immediate feelings and effects

Follow Up

Manifestation Date _____

Results _____

Date _____ Caster _____

Name of Ritual or Spell _____

Purpose _____

Participants   Deities Invoked

| Waxing | | | Full Moon | | Waning | |

Description		Ingredients and Equipment

Immediate feelings and effects		

Follow Up

Manifestation Date _____

Results _____

Date _____   Caster _____

Name of Ritual or Spell _____

Purpose _____

Participants   **Deities Invoked**

| Waxing | | | Full Moon | | | Waning |

Description

Ingredients and Equipment

Immediate feelings and effects

Follow Up

Manifestation Date _____

Results _____

Date _____ Caster _____

Name of Ritual or Spell _____

Purpose _____

Participants   Deities Invoked

Waxing	Full Moon	Waning

Description

Ingredients and Equipment

Immediate feelings and effects

Follow Up

Manifestation Date _____

Results _____

Date _____ Caster _____

Name of Ritual or Spell _____

Purpose _____

Participants   Deities Invoked

Waxing   Full Moon   Waning

Description

Ingredients and Equipment

Immediate feelings and effects

Follow Up

Manifestation Date _____

Results _____

Date _____ Caster _____

Name of Ritual or Spell _____

Purpose _____

Participants   Deities Invoked

Waxing	Full Moon	Waning

Description

Ingredients and Equipment

Immediate feelings and effects

Follow Up

Manifestation Date _____

Results _____

Date _____ Caster _____

Name of Ritual or Spell _____

Purpose _____

Participants   Deities Invoked

Waxing   Full Moon   Waning

Description

Ingredients and Equipment

Immediate feelings and effects

Follow Up

Manifestation Date _____

Results _____

Date _____   Caster _____

Name of Ritual or Spell _____

Purpose _____

Participants   Deities Invoked

| Waxing | Full Moon | Waning |

Description

Ingredients and Equipment

Immediate feelings and effects

Follow Up

Manifestation Date _____

Results _____

Date _____ Caster _____

Name of Ritual or Spell _____

Purpose _____

Participants   **Deities Invoked**

| Waxing | Full Moon | Waning |

Description

Ingredients and Equipment

Immediate feelings and effects

Follow Up

Manifestation Date _____

Results _____

Date _____ Caster _____

Name of Ritual or Spell _____

Purpose _____

Participants   Deities Invoked

Waxing	Full Moon	Waning

Description

Ingredients and Equipment

Immediate feelings and effects

Follow Up

Manifestation Date _____

Results _____

Date _____ Caster _____

Name of Ritual or Spell _____

Purpose _____

Participants **Deities Invoked**

Waxing   Full Moon   Waning

Description

Ingredients and Equipment

Immediate feelings and effects

Follow Up

Manifestation Date _____

Results _____

Date _____ Caster _____

Name of Ritual or Spell _____

Purpose _____

Participants   **Deities Invoked**

Waxing	Full Moon	Waning

Description

Ingredients and Equipment

Immediate feelings and effects

Follow Up

Manifestation Date _____

Results _____

Date _____   Caster _____

Name of Ritual or Spell _____

Purpose _____

Participants   **Deities Invoked**

Waxing	Full Moon	Waning

Description

Ingredients and Equipment

Immediate feelings and effects

Follow Up

Manifestation Date _____

Results _____

Date _____ Caster _____

Name of Ritual or Spell _____

Purpose _____

Participants   Deities Invoked

| Waxing | Full Moon | Waning |

Description

Ingredients and Equipment

Immediate feelings and effects

Follow Up

Manifestation Date _____

Results _____

Date _____   Caster _____

Name of Ritual or Spell _____

Purpose _____

Participants   **Deities Invoked**

| Waxing | Full Moon | Waning |

Description

Ingredients and Equipment

Immediate feelings and effects

Follow Up

Manifestation Date _____

Results _____

Date _____ Caster _____

Name of Ritual or Spell _____

Purpose _____

Participants   **Deities Invoked**

Waxing   Full Moon   Waning

Description

Ingredients and Equipment

Immediate feelings and effects

Follow Up

Manifestation Date _____

Results _____

Date _____ Caster _____

Name of Ritual or Spell _____

Purpose _____

Participants   **Deities Invoked**

| Waxing   Full Moon   Waning |

Description

Ingredients and Equipment

Immediate feelings and effects

Follow Up

Manifestation Date _____

Results _____

Date _____ Caster _____

Name of Ritual or Spell _____

Purpose _____

Participants   **Deities Invoked**

Waxing	Full Moon	Waning

Description

Ingredients and Equipment

Immediate feelings and effects

Follow Up

Manifestation Date _____

Results _____

Date _____   Caster _____

Name of Ritual or Spell _____

Purpose _____

Participants   **Deities Invoked**

Waxing	Full Moon	Waning

Description
_____
_____
_____
_____

Ingredients and Equipment
_____
_____
_____
_____
_____
_____
_____
_____

Immediate feelings and effects
_____
_____
_____
_____
_____

Follow Up

Manifestation Date _____

Results _____

Date _____   Caster _____

Name of Ritual or Spell _____

Purpose _____

Participants   Deities Invoked

| Waxing | Full Moon | Waning |

Description

Ingredients and Equipment

Immediate feelings and effects

Follow Up

Manifestation Date _____

Results _____

Date _____ Caster _____

Name of Ritual or Spell _____

Purpose _____

Participants **Deities Invoked**

Waxing	Full Moon	Waning

Description

Ingredients and Equipment

Immediate feelings and effects

Follow Up

Manifestation Date _____

Results _____

Date _____ Caster _____

Name of Ritual or Spell _____

Purpose _____

Participants   Deities Invoked

Waxing	Full Moon	Waning

Description

Ingredients and Equipment

Immediate feelings and effects

Follow Up

Manifestation Date _____

Results _____

Date _____ Caster _____

Name of Ritual or Spell _____

Purpose _____

Participants   Deities Invoked

| Waxing | Full Moon | Waning |

Description

Ingredients and Equipment

Immediate feelings and effects

Follow Up

Manifestation Date _____

Results _____

Date _____ Caster _____

Name of Ritual or Spell _____

Purpose _____

Participants   Deities Invoked

Waxing	Full Moon	Waning

Description

Ingredients and Equipment

Immediate feelings and effects

Follow Up

Manifestation Date _____

Results _____

Date _____ Caster _____

Name of Ritual or Spell _____

Purpose _____

Participants   **Deities Invoked**

Waxing	Full Moon	Waning

Description

Ingredients and Equipment

Immediate feelings and effects

Follow Up

Manifestation Date _____

Results _____

Date _____ Caster _____

Name of Ritual or Spell _____

Purpose _____

Participants **Deities Invoked**

| Waxing | Full Moon | Waning |

Description

Ingredients and Equipment

Immediate feelings and effects

Follow Up

Manifestation Date _____

Results _____

Date _____   Caster _____

Name of Ritual or Spell _____

Purpose _____

Participants   **Deities Invoked**

Waxing	Full Moon	Waning

Description

Ingredients and Equipment

Immediate feelings and effects

Follow Up

Manifestation Date _____

Results _____

Date _____ Caster _____

Name of Ritual or Spell _____

Purpose _____

Participants   Deities Invoked

| Waxing | Full Moon | Waning |

Description

Ingredients and Equipment

Immediate feelings and effects

Follow Up

Manifestation Date _____

Results _____

Date _____ Caster _____

Name of Ritual or Spell _____

Purpose _____

Participants   **Deities Invoked**

Waxing	Full Moon	Waning

Description

Ingredients and Equipment

Immediate feelings and effects

Follow Up

Manifestation Date _____

Results _____

Date _____ Caster _____

Name of Ritual or Spell _____

Purpose _____

Participants   Deities Invoked

Waxing	Full Moon	Waning

Description

Ingredients and Equipment

Immediate feelings and effects

Follow Up

Manifestation Date _____

Results _____

Date _____   Caster _____

Name of Ritual or Spell _____

Purpose _____

Participants   Deities Invoked

| Waxing | Full Moon | Waning |

Description

Ingredients and Equipment

Immediate feelings and effects

Follow Up

Manifestation Date _____

Results _____

Date _____ Caster _____

Name of Ritual or Spell _____

Purpose _____

Participants   Deities Invoked

| Waxing | Full Moon | Waning |

Description

Ingredients and Equipment

Immediate feelings and effects

Follow Up

Manifestation Date _____

Results _____

Date _____ Caster _____

Name of Ritual or Spell _____

Purpose _____

Participants   **Deities Invoked**

Waxing   Full Moon   Waning

Description

Ingredients and Equipment

Immediate feelings and effects

Follow Up

Manifestation Date _____

Results _____

Date _____ Caster _____

Name of Ritual or Spell _____

Purpose _____

Participants   Deities Invoked

Waxing	Full Moon	Waning

Description

Ingredients and Equipment

Immediate feelings and effects

Follow Up

Manifestation Date _____

Results _____

Date _____   Caster _____

Name of Ritual or Spell _____

Purpose _____

Participants   Deities Invoked

| Waxing | Full Moon | Waning |

Description

Ingredients and Equipment

Immediate feelings and effects

Follow Up

Manifestation Date _____

Results _____

Date _____ Caster _____

Name of Ritual or Spell _____

Purpose _____

Participants   Deities Invoked

Waxing	Full Moon	Waning

Description

Ingredients and Equipment

Immediate feelings and effects

Follow Up

Manifestation Date _____

Results _____

Date _____ Caster _____

Name of Ritual or Spell _____

Purpose _____

Participants   **Deities Invoked**

| Waxing | Full Moon | Waning |

Description

Ingredients and Equipment

Immediate feelings and effects

Follow Up

Manifestation Date _____

Results _____

Date _____ Caster _____

Name of Ritual or Spell _____

Purpose _____

Participants   Deities Invoked

| Waxing | Full Moon | Waning |

Description

Ingredients and Equipment

Immediate feelings and effects

Follow Up

Manifestation Date _____

Results _____

Date _____ Caster _____

Name of Ritual or Spell _____

Purpose _____

Participants **Deities Invoked**

Waxing	Full Moon	Waning

Description

Ingredients and Equipment

Immediate feelings and effects

Follow Up

Manifestation Date _____

Results _____

Date _____   **Caster** _____

Name of Ritual or Spell _____

Purpose _____

Participants   Deities Invoked

| Waxing | Full Moon | Waning |

Description

Ingredients and Equipment

Immediate feelings and effects

Follow Up

Manifestation Date _____

Results _____

Date _____ Caster _____

Name of Ritual or Spell _____

Purpose _____

Participants   **Deities Invoked**

| Waxing | Full Moon | Waning |

Description

Ingredients and Equipment

Immediate feelings and effects

Follow Up

Manifestation Date _____

Results _____

Date _____ Caster _____

Name of Ritual or Spell _____

Purpose _____

Participants   Deities Invoked

| Waxing | Full Moon | Waning |

Description

Ingredients and Equipment

Immediate feelings and effects

Follow Up

Manifestation Date _____

Results _____

Date _____ Caster _____

Name of Ritual or Spell _____

Purpose _____

Participants   Deities Invoked

| Waxing | Full Moon | Waning |

Description

Ingredients and Equipment

Immediate feelings and effects

Follow Up

Manifestation Date _____

Results _____

Date _____   Caster _____

Name of Ritual or Spell _____

Purpose _____

Participants   Deities Invoked

Waxing   Full Moon   Waning

Description

Ingredients and Equipment

Immediate feelings and effects

Follow Up

Manifestation Date _____

Results _____

Date _____   Caster _____

Name of Ritual or Spell _____

Purpose _____

Participants   **Deities Invoked**

Waxing   Full Moon   Waning

Description

Ingredients and Equipment

Immediate feelings and effects

Follow Up

Manifestation Date _____

Results _____

Date _____ Caster _____

Name of Ritual or Spell _____

Purpose _____

Participants   Deities Invoked

Waxing	Full Moon	Waning

Description

Ingredients and Equipment

Immediate feelings and effects

Follow Up

Manifestation Date _____

Results _____

Date _____ Caster _____

Name of Ritual or Spell _____

Purpose _____

Participants   **Deities Invoked**

Waxing	Full Moon	Waning

Description

Ingredients and Equipment

Immediate feelings and effects

Follow Up

Manifestation Date _____

Results _____

Date _____ Caster _____

Name of Ritual or Spell _____

Purpose _____

Participants   Deities Invoked

Waxing	Full Moon	Waning

Description

Ingredients and Equipment

Immediate feelings and effects

Follow Up

Manifestation Date _____

Results _____

Date _____   Caster _____

Name of Ritual or Spell _____

Purpose _____

Participants   **Deities Invoked**

| Waxing | | | Full Moon | | Waning | |

Description

Ingredients and Equipment

Immediate feelings and effects

Follow Up

Manifestation Date _____

Results _____

Date _____   Caster _____

Name of Ritual or Spell _____

Purpose _____

Participants   Deities Invoked

Waxing   Full Moon   Waning

Description

Ingredients and Equipment

Immediate feelings and effects

Follow Up

Manifestation Date _____

Results _____

Date _____   Caster _____

Name of Ritual or Spell _____

Purpose _____

Participants   **Deities Invoked**

| Waxing | Full Moon | Waning |

Description

Ingredients and Equipment

Immediate feelings and effects

Follow Up

Manifestation Date _____

Results _____

Date _____ Caster _____

Name of Ritual or Spell _____

Purpose _____

Participants   Deities Invoked

| Waxing | Full Moon | Waning |

Description

Ingredients and Equipment

Immediate feelings and effects

Follow Up

Manifestation Date _____

Results _____

Date _____ Caster _____

Name of Ritual or Spell _____

Purpose _____

Participants   Deities Invoked

| Waxing | Full Moon | Waning |

Description

Ingredients and Equipment

Immediate feelings and effects

Follow Up

Manifestation Date _____

Results _____

Date _____ Caster _____

Name of Ritual or Spell _____

Purpose _____

Participants   Deities Invoked

| Waxing | Full Moon | Waning |

Description

_____
_____
_____
_____
_____

Ingredients and Equipment

_____
_____
_____
_____
_____
_____
_____
_____
_____

Immediate feelings and effects

_____
_____
_____
_____
_____

Follow Up

Manifestation Date _____

Results _____

Date _____ Caster _____

Name of Ritual or Spell _____

Purpose _____

Participants **Deities Invoked**

Waxing   Full Moon   Waning

Description

Ingredients and Equipment

Immediate feelings and effects

Follow Up

Manifestation Date _____

Results _____

www.ingramcontent.com/pod-product-compliance
Ingram Content Group UK Ltd.
Pitfield, Milton Keynes, MK11 3LW, UK
UKHW022223230426
12048UKWH00016␣A/1022